# INTIMATE ENCOUNTERS OF WORSHIP

*The King of Glory Shall Come In*

Darrell D. Kelly

Author's Tranquility Press
ATLANTA, GEORGIA

Copyright © 2023 by Darrell D. Kelly

All rights reserved. No part of this publication may be reproduced, distributed or transmitted in any form or by any means, including photocopying, recording, or other electronic or mechanical methods, without the prior written permission of the publisher, except in the case of brief quotations embodied in critical reviews and certain other noncommercial uses permitted by copyright law. For permission requests, write to the publisher, addressed "Attention: Permissions Coordinator," at the address below.

Darrell D. Kelly/Author's Tranquility Press
3800 Camp Creek Pkwy SW Bldg. 1400-116 #1255
Atlanta, GA 30331, USA
www.authorstranquilitypress.com

Ordering Information:
Quantity sales. Special discounts are available on quantity purchases by corporations, associations, and others. For details, contact the "Special Sales Department" at the address above.

Intimate Encounters of Worship / Darrell D. Kelly
Paperback: 978-1-962859-16-5
eBook: 978-1-962859-17-2

# Contents

Forword ............................................................................................i

Chapter 1: "Ye know Not Who You Worship!" .....................1

   God of Peace ...............................................................................3

   The All-Knowing God ...............................................................3

   God is Creator and Maker of All ............................................4

   Did God Create Evil? ................................................................5

   God Is Love .................................................................................8

   The Purified Heart and Vessels of Honor .........................16

      "Regaining the Respect for God's Power" ....................20

Chapter 2: "From the Well to Worship" ................................26

      "Give Me To Drink" ............................................................27

      "The Gift of God" ................................................................29

      "Are You Greater?" ..............................................................31

      "Go, Call Your Husband" ..................................................35

      "You Don't Know What You Worship" .........................39

      "In spirt and in truth" ..........................................................47

Chapter 3: "Lifestyle of Radical Worship" ............................51

Chapter 4: "The King of Glory Shall Come In" ..................70

Chapter 5: "Worship the King" ................................................87

Chapter 6: "The Conclusion" ...................................................93

# Forword

Many anointed men and women of God have decreed the year 2020 to be a year of 20/20 Vision, which represents perfect vision, the best, a year in which seeing through the eyes of God is not only relevant, but mandatory. As Christian believers, if our eyes are fixed on the world all around us and its foundations that seem to be crumbling at an accelerated pace, what we actually see in real time can become overwhelmingly stressful and even cause panic. It is in times like these, we all need a fresh voice sent from God who will tag us by our jackets with a fresh and accurate word from God that draws our focus back toward God and His purpose! He has a plan, and even when we cannot trace Him, we must learn to fully trust Him!!

Darrell Kelly is one of those resounding voices God is using in this millennium to draw our collective attention back to what really matters. He has something to say and the integrity to say it. In this book he challenges thoughts and brings insights that will stir the hearing hearts with a hunger for more. We are created for God's purpose and plan in this time and place. I believe we each are genetically accurate, geographically precise, and chronologically correct for the assignment we've been given.

You may ask, "Why this book when so many others are on the horizon?" I highly recommend this book as a tool that not only addresses elements of and approaches to worship, but presents incisive thought to prepare the worshiper! As a lyric in one of my songs says, "Let our hearts seek your face, oh Lord, and not just your hand, dear Lord; with every breath that we breath, to pursue our destiny." Having known Darrell Kelly all of his life, I have seen the hand of God upon Him, as with his parents before him. The privilege of watching a young musician being sculpted into a devoted prophet, pastor and teacher, was given to me. What a blessing! And most of all, you will enjoy the journey.

*Helena Barrington*

*My Utmost for HIS Highest!*

# Chapter 1:

## "Ye know Not Who You Worship!"

If I were to ask you who God is, what would you say? Do you really know who God is? What can you tell me about God? Well of course, those of us who have some knowledge of the Bible and profess to be a believer of the scriptures, would most often say the following:

* God is Jehovah-Jirah (The Lord our Provider) according to Genesis 22:14

* God is Jehovah-Nissi (The Lord our Banner in Victory) according to Exodus 17:15

* God is Jehovah-Ropheka (The Lord our Healer) according to Exodus 15:26

* God is Jehovah-Shalom (The Lord our Peace) according to Judges 6:24

* God is Jehovah-Shammah (The Lord Is There) according to Ezekiel 48:35

In response to the same opening questions, others would include in addition to the names of Jehovah, that God is:

* Elohim, El Shaddi

* Yah/Yahweh

* Adoni

Even beyond this second list many responses have been these:

* God is Creator and Maker of all things

* God is Love

* God is All Powerful (omnipotent)

* God is All Knowing (omniscient)

* God is everywhere at once (omnipresent)

Just for a moment, let us explore and confirm some of these responses to who God is. Although these descriptions of God are very true there is yet another side of God that we tend to overlook. And it is that aspect of God's character that I wish to challenge you with to some degree as we begin this journey.

## _God of Peace_

The Bible addresses God as the God of peace in Hebrews 13:20-21 (KJV), where is states:

*20.) Now the God of peace, that brought again from the dead our Lord Jesus, that great shepherd of the sheep, through the blood of everlasting covenant,*

*21.) Make you perfect in every good work to do his will, working in you that which is well pleasing in his sight, through Jesus Christ, to whom be glory for ever and ever.*

Not only is God a God of Peace, his Son Jesus Christ is the Prince of Peace according to Isaiah 9:6-7.

## _The All-Knowing God_

As the Lord speaks in the book of Isaiah (46:9-10 KJV), we realize that there is in fact nothing that God doesn't know:

*9.) Remember the former things of old: for I am God and there is none else; I am God, and there is none like me,*

***10.) Declaring the end form the beginning, and form ancient times the things that are not yet done, saying, my counsel shall stand, and I will do all my pleasure.***

God is all knowing. God can declare what the end will be from the beginning. He sees the finish before the start. I like to compare this to an artist who sees in his mind what the painting will look like even before he begins to paint. Or the songwriter who hears in his heart what the song will sound like before it is ever recorded. Gods' ability to know everything is absolutely amazing!

## *God is Creator and Maker of All*

God being known as "Maker" and "Creator" is one of the more wide spread views in the Christian faith of who God is. Even in other religions and beliefs God is defined or known as "The Creator." In the book of St. John, we are shown that God made all things. (God through His Word).

***John 1:1-3 (KJV)***

***1.) In the beginning was the Word, and the Word was with god and the Word was God.***

***2.) The same was in the beginning with God.***

*3.) <u>All things were made by him</u>; and without him was not anything made that was made.*

The Bible also declares in Isaiah 44:24 (KJV);

*24.) Thus saith the Lord thy redeemer, and he that formed thee in the womb<u>, I am the Lord that maketh all things</u>; that stretcheth forth the heavens alone; and spreadeth abroad the earth by myself;*

Based upon the Bible as the infallible Word of God; God is in fact Creator and Maker of all things. Therefore, if I were to ask "did God create all things?" Most people would say yes. Of course, if I were to ask if there was anything that God didn't create, most answers would be, no. However, now I pose a new question and thought before you:

## *<u>Did God Create Evil?</u>*

There is a familiar phrase in our western church world that goes as follows: "God is good, all the time and all the time, God is Good." I am pretty sure that we all would agree that God is good. No one would be inspired to worship, honor and serve a "bad" God. But I ask you; if God created everything does that mean he create evil? To answer this question, we must examine Isaiah 45:5-7 (KJV):

*5.) I am the Lord, and there is none else, there is no God beside me: I girded thee, though thou hast not known me:*

*6.) That they may know form the rising of the sun, and form the west, that there is none beside me. I am the Lord and there is none else.*

*7.) I form the light, and create darkness: <u>I make peace, and create evil</u>: I the Lord do all these things.*

Whenever I preach on this subject, the audience always has that "I can't believe it" expression on their faces. All of a sudden people are faced with a feeling of uncertainty of whom they "thought" God was. It is too hard to imagine that our "Good God" would be capable of such evil actions. Well, believe or not God admits to us in scripture that he created evil.

I know what you are thinking, maybe if we defined the word evil then that would make a difference. Well, okay let's try it:

**Evil** – (Hebrew: Ra) meaning: Bad or Badness

**Evil** – Is also translated to be: Disaster, Calamity, or Destruction

No matter how we look at it or define it, "Evil" still doesn't get any better. Nor does it take away the fact that it is the Lord who does all these things. The very thought and truth of God being the initiator of "evil events" seems so contrary to what we are accustomed to hearing from preachers in the pulpits across the nation. When the United States first experienced the terrorist attack on September 11th 2001; I began to really seek God to know what was and is happening in the spiritual realm. Think back in time with me. Even today that great act of disaster and destruction was not that long ago. Many lives were lost; many who are alive still suffer loss, and the nation as a whole suffered great losses.

So, in light of the destructive disaster we have witnessed on our nation's soil, the possibilities of future attacks; and the calamity that continues to rage in many other nations, **is it safe to say that God created this evil?** How can you really know the truth from one preacher on TV who says that this was Gods' judgment on America because of sin, when another preacher says that it was not an act of God but rather the work of evil men? Where do we draw the line? Who's right? Who's wrong? Who do we trust? Who do we believe? Is God responsible or is man responsible? Is it an accident or just a sign of the end of the world drawing near? It is amazing that the deeper we dig into knowing who God is, the less comfortable we become with what we thought we already knew about God. Perhaps we really don't know...in whom we worship. I understand, however, that since God is so Great, Awesome, and Mighty it would be impossible for us with limited human ability to know him completely in every aspect of his Divine Deity.

## *God Is Love*

*1 John 4:7-8 (KJV) reads:*

*7.) Beloved, let us love one another: for love is of God; and every one that loveth is born of God, and knoweth God.*

*8.) "He that loveth not knoweth not God; for <u>God is love</u>.*

Isn't it good to know that God is love? God doesn't just give love; God is love! God loved the world so much that he gave his only Son to bring us salvation and eternal life. (John 3:16-17) I found it interesting that John 3:16 begins with, "For God so loved the world," because the question came to me asking; "Does God love every one?" I thought just as many others that because God loved the world, that meant he loved everyone in the world. After all, the Bible declares that it is God's will that none should perish (2 Peter 3:9). Ponder that for a moment; is there anyone that God doesn't love? Before you answer that question with a "no" let's look in the scriptures.

*Romans 9:9-13 (KJV)*

*9.) For this is the word of promise, at this time will I come, and Sarah shall conceive a son.*

*10.) And not only this; but when Rebecca also had conceived by one, even by our father Isaac:*

*11.) (For the children being not yet born, neither having done any good or evil, that the purpose of God according to election might stand, not of works, but of him that calleth;)*

*12.) It was said unto her, The elder shall server the younger.*

*13.) As it is written, <u>Jacob have I loved, but Esau have I hated</u>.*

Now, hold on just one minute, are you telling me that God would love one person and hate the other? Does not the Bible say in *Acts 10:34* that **"God is no respecter of persons?"** How can this be, seeing that they were only children in the womb of their mother Rebecca, having done no good or evil? Is this right?

Is this fair? I have often heard it mentioned that God loves the sinner but hates the sin. However, in this text of scripture, God hates someone who has not committed a sin. Understandably, someone's response may be that God hated Esau because of some future action, or future sin; something that Esau would eventually do to offend God. If that were the case, it still would not be valid because we all were born with a nature to sin. God knows everyone's future and there will continually be sins that we commit; even with good intentions. So, tell me, since God knows everything about our past, present, and future, what keeps him from hating us all?

Let's continue reading in Romans 9:14 (KJV)

14.) ***What shall we say then? Is there unrighteousness with God? God forbid.***

Note: Be careful that you don't accuse God of being unjust or unrighteous.

> *14.) For he sayeth to Moses, I will have mercy on whom I will have mercy, and I will have compassion on whom I will have compassion.*
>
> *15.) So then it not of him that willeth, nor of him that runneth, but of God that showeth mercy.*

Verse 16 communicates to us the fact that God's mercy toward us is not contingent upon our will and what we will to do; nor is it based upon "him that runs" or one who exerts his own effort to merit special favor from God. The truth is that we only receive mercy and compassion from God because he makes the decision to give it to us. There is absolutely no work, deed, or action that we can do, express, or perform to invoke the mercy of God into our lives! Simply put, to answer why God would do what he does is that "GOD IS IN CONTROL!"

## *Romans 9:17 (KJV)*

> *14.) For the scripture saith unto Pharaoh, even <u>for this same purpose have I raised thee up, that I might show my power in thee</u>, and that my name might be declared throughout all the earth.*

God's only purpose for raising up a hard-hearted Pharaoh, who enslaved the children of Israel in more harsh conditions for several years, was to destroy him and show his power that His Name might be declared in all the earth. Does God still raise up people for the purpose of destroying them? Many Christians today seem to have no real awareness of how much control the Lord really has. There is a casual since of familiarity to God, rather than a fear and reverence of God. In many ways in our western church culture, we have lost respect for the "Awesomeness of God!"

*Romans 9:18 (KJV)*

*14.) Therefore he hath mercy on whom he will have mercy, and whom he will he hardeneth.*

Why would God send Moses to tell Pharaoh to let His people go, if God was going to be the one to harden the heart of Pharaoh to keep him from letting the people go? (Exodus 4:20-21) The Bible makes it clear that it was in fact the Lord who hardened the heart of Pharaoh. However, as we have read in Romans, God has mercy or hardens whom he wills.

*Romans 9:19 (KJV)*

*19.) Thou wilt say then unto me, why doth he yet find fault? For who has resisted his will?*

In other words, how can God blame us or hold us responsible for our condition, if he's the one who chooses and controls whether or not we can receive him or reject him? If God created me, and God created evil (which he did) but knowing all things - he knew that I would do evil...How, therefore, can God hold me accountable for the evil that I do if he made me to do it? If my condition is based upon

God's will, how can I resist his will? Interesting isn't it? This is the mentality of many people who attempt to support their lifestyle of sin by using scripture as consent or permission. During the rise of the gay and lesbian movement here in the U.S. two of the phrases I heard quite often from them was "God made me this way" or "I was born this way." I have heard the alcoholic say, "even Jesus drunk wine." Why are we so comfortable with unrighteousness? Of course, if we can convince ourselves that our condition is because of God, then we have justification to live unholy, yet religiously.

*Romans 9:20-21*

*20.) Nay but, O man, who art thou that repliest against God? Shall the thing formed say to him that formed it, why hast thou made me thus?*

*21.) Hath not the potter power over the clay, of the same lump to make one vessel unto honor, and another unto dishonor?*

Does not the potter have power over the clay to make what he wants? Isn't God in control of what he makes? Yes, He Is, therefore who are we to challenge and/or to criticize God? Who are we to set our mouth against what God has done? God has made vessels of honor as well as vessels of dishonor. I often liken this to dinnerware, in that vessels of honor would be the fine china or crystal glasses and the vessels of dishonor would be the disposable plastic cups. The vessels of honor are held in safe places for special occasions; whereas the vessels of dishonor can be discarded at any time. However, every now and then we have "mercy on a vessel of dishonor" by washing it out and keeping it longer instead of immediately throwing it away after use. Look at how God does the same with us.

*Romans 9:22-24*

*22.) What if God, willing to show his wrath, and to make his power known, endured with much longsuffering the vessels of wrath fitted to destruction.*

*23.) And that he might make known the riches of his glory on the vessels of mercy, which he had afore prepared unto glory,*

*24.) Even us, whom he hath called, not of the Jews only, but also of the Gentiles?*

The main idea behind this opening, "Ye know not who you worship" section of the book is to help you realize that the more you meditate on the power and mercy of God, the less control you realize that you have. You may be a free moral agent, but you are not as free as you think; God is in control! Do you realize that God even controls when you get saved? Hear the words of Jesus as he addressed the Jews who murmured at his teaching in the book of John.

*John 6:44 (KJV)*

*44.) No man can come unto me, <u>except the Father which hath sent me draw him</u>: and I will raise him up at the last day.*

God so sovereign that He chooses when He'll draw you to Christ. Be careful that your relationship and worship to God is not based upon the blessings you believe you can receive from him; but based upon the fact that he chose you when he didn't have to. He called you when he was not required to. He drew you unto himself when he not obligated to. Because of sin, we were all guilty and should have faced the punishment and penalty of death as eternal separation from God! If you are reading this book right now, God has shown mercy to you. Take this time to repent, turn away from, and renounce any evil or unrighteous ways in your life; then take time to give God praise for his mercy, compassion, longsuffering, and willingness draw you unto himself. GOD IS IN CONTROL!

## *The Purified Heart and Vessels of Honor*

*2 Timothy 2:19-20 (KJV)*

*19.) Never the less the foundation of god standeth sure, having this seal, The Lord knoweth them that are his. And let everyone that nameth the name of Christ depart from iniquity.*

*20.) But in a great house there are not only vessels of gold and of silver, but also of wood and earth; and some to honor, and some to dishonor.*

We have already discussed the power of God's control to choose whether or not we receive mercy and compassion. God chooses when to draw us unto salvation. God chooses when to judge us. God chooses when to prosper us. God chooses when to lift us up or bring us down. By now you may have wondered exactly where you stand in the eyes of God? A valid question to ask yourself is, "How can I know for certain where I am with God"

*2 Timothy 2:21 (KJV)*

*If a man therefore purge himself from these, <u>he shall be a vessel unto honor</u>, sanctified, and meet for the master's use, and prepared unto every good work.*

**The key to becoming a vessel of honor is purification!** A person must be able to "purge himself" to be a vessel of honor. This is not the purging that God does for you, but this is the purging that you do to yourself. The blood of Jesus Christ purges us from unrighteousness and cleanses our spiritual man, blotting out our sins; but spiritual discipline and Godly character purges us from the works of the flesh and carnality.

*2 Timothy 2:22 (KJV)*

*22.) Flee also youthful lusts: but follow righteousness, faith, charity, peace, with them that call on the Lord out of a pure heart.*

Verses 21 and 22 in this passage of scripture give us the insight to how we become vessels of dishonor as well. If we do not purge our lives, we will become vessels of dishonor. Nor if we refuse to flee the youthful lusts that come to distract us from pursuing or following after righteousness, faith, love, and peace. Without the purging process, we will not be able to call on the Lord out of a "Pure Heart." The youthful lusts have taken our focus from wanting purification, and placed it upon wanting a blessing. To many Christians, especially in our western culture desire the new home, car, or some increase of money "more" than they desire to be purified before God.

* We say we love God but our attitude is filthy!

* We say we love God but our commitment is weak!

* We say we love God but we just want His "stuff."

We want blessings from him more than we want the right relationship with him. Too often in our lives, our worship and relationship with God is based upon the severity of our needs rather than the inspiration to commune intimately with the "Father." It is this type of lifestyle that causes one to be categorized as a vessel of dishonor in the eyes of God.

In your life, at this present time the Lord has chosen to show mercy on you. He has endured with us much longsuffering as the vessels fitted unto destruction. Although the Lord reserves complete control of all creation, He is gracious enough to give us the ability to choose whether or not we will be vessels of honor or vessels of dishonor.

*Ezekiel 11:19-21 (KJV)*

*19.) And I will give them one heart, and I will put a new spirit within you; and I will take the stony heart out of their flesh, and will give them an heart of flesh;*

God desires to take away the heart that is hardened towards his ways, and exchange it for a heart that is sensitive to moving of his spirit and responsive to his touch.

*20.) That they may walk in my statutes, and keep mine ordinances, and do them: and they shall be my people, and I will be their God.*

*21.) But as for them whose heart walketh after the heart of their detestable things and their abominations, I will recompense their way upon their own heads, saith the Lord.*

There are many people claiming to be children of God who yet choose to hold fast to their impure hearts. This heart houses that which is detestable and is an abomination to God. Therefore, by choosing to keep the impure heart, God may very well reward you by allowing you to become captive, trapped or enslaved by the impurity of your own heart. Thus, allowing you to experience and be exposed to the fullness of the evil that lies within your own unchanged heart. This is why it is vital for us as believers to purge ourselves and cleanse our ways, wash our hands, and purify our hearts. This is the way to become vessels of honor.

## "Regaining the Respect for God's Power"

The problem that I see in our modern church era is the lack of respect for God's Power. There is no genuine "Fear of the Lord" in our congregations.

For example, I know a few people that are employed by the power company and work at the power plant in my city. In their day-to-day lives, they are not afraid of electricity, mainly because they use electricity on a daily basis. Electricity powers our lights, appliances, heaters, air conditions, tools, machines, and so much more. For the most part, we are not afraid of electricity because it has become a normal part of our daily lives. However, when the power plant workers are on duty in the power plant they are exposed to the massive generators, extremely powerful turbine engines, heat, and chemicals, just to give you an idea. In this power plant environment, any procedure being performed must be done correctly with careful attention to the regulations, guidelines, inspections, and safety.

The reason so much care and training are required, is because we know what can happen to a human being if all of that "power" is released against or into a person's body. We are not afraid of electricity but we **"respect its power."** The electricity released has the capacity to either assist you or destroy you. Even in homes and schools, children are taught not to place their fingers and objects into electrical outlets; not because we fear electricity itself; but we understand that it has the power to destroy. We love the fact that God has the power to bless, heal, help, and love us; but we tend to forget that God still has the power to destroy. Therefore, I hear in my spirit, the Lord saying that; "if you commit to following after me, then follow me completely! Because you could be raised up like pharaoh and my power turned against you!"

I know that some may argue the point that we are not living under Law of the Old Testament but rather the Grace of the New Testament, and that God would not (or does not) destroy men today as he did in the days of old. I believe that thus far I have maintained a good balance of Old and New Testament scriptures and references to support these aspects of the character of God, however, let us examine a New Testament example of this truth.

**Acts 5:1-5 (KJV)**

Read verses 1 through 11 for the entire story.

1.) *But a certain man named Ananias, with Sapphira his wife, sold a possession,*

2.) *And kept back part of the price, his wife also being privy to it, and brought a certain part and laid it at the apostles' feet.*

3.) *But Peter said, Ananias, Why hath Satan filled thine heart to lie to the Holy Ghost, and to keep back part of the price of the land?*

4.) *Whiles it remained, was it not thine own? And after it was sold, was it not in thine own power? Why hast thou conceived this thin in thine heart? Thou hast not lied unto men, but unto God.*

5.) *And Ananias hearing those words fell down, and gave up the ghost; and great fear came upon all them that heard these things.*

Here's the situation, Ananias along with his wife sold a piece of land at a certain price. After selling the property, they withheld a certain amount for themselves. Then when they had brought it to before the apostles as an offering, Ananias and his wife being involved with this scheme, presented the money as if it were the whole amount, knowing that they had kept back a part of the price.

Many of us as Christians are reflections of the modern-day Ananias, in that there are areas of our lives in which we hold back from God. We may sing songs such as "I surrender all" but in reality, we have not surrendered all! We honestly haven't given God 100% of who we are, what we do, or what we face in life. We try to present ourselves before God as if we have given our all and given our best when in actuality we lie to the Holy Ghost because we keep back a part of the price for ourselves.

Romans chapter 12 verse 1 tells us that we should present our bodies as a living and holy sacrifice. The life of the believer is to be a life of complete sacrificial surrender unto the Lord. It is because of the Lord that we exist. It is in Him that we live, move and have our being, and by His power our life is sustained. Everything that we have is really His. "The earth is the Lord's and the fullness thereof; the world, and they that dwell therein." (Psalm 24:1). We are not owners; we are merely stewards; and our responsibility is not to ourselves but unto God. Think about how many decisions you've made, how many places to which you've traveled, or how many things you've done without praying about it first, then awaiting God's response. Most of what we do is based on our own ability to do for ourselves and not based on finding and fulfilling God's will. **Be careful about presenting yourself before God, without presenting the "Whole Price."**

Peter asked the question to Ananias that I also ask you. Why has Satan filled your heart to lie to the Holy Ghost? Some of you didn't know that as a believer Satan could fill your heart, but it's true. There again is the reason that we continually purge ourselves and walk in purity of heart. Don't think for a moment that because you believe in God you automatically become an acceptable living sacrifice unto God.

Ananias along with his wife fell dead in the midst of the saints as a result of their dishonesty to the Holy Ghost. It is very important that you realize that in the New Testament church, God still reserves the right to destroy vessels of dishonor. The "Fear of the Lord" must return to the hearts of the children of God. People don't take church seriously because they don't fear the Lord. Young people think that they have time to fool around before getting serious about God because they don't fear the Lord. Christians will lie, cheat, and steal just like the unsaved because they don't fear the Lord. People who profess to be children of God will deal deceitfully and dishonestly having no integrity or regard for others because they don't fear the Lord.

You see, the fear of the Lord is not about being scared or afraid of God but it is when you realize that God doesn't "have to" have you; and you choose to walk uprightly, and circumspectly, with respect for his power.

Maintaining respect for God's power is the beginning of wisdom and the process of perfecting holiness in the fear of God.

# Chapter 2:

## "From the Well to Worship"

*John 4:1-30 (KJV)*

*1.) When therefore the Lord knew how the Pharisees had heard that Jesus made and baptized more disciples than John,*

*2.) (Though Jesus himself baptized not, but his disciples,)*

*3.) He left Judaea, and departed again into Galilee.*

*4.) And he must needs go through Samaria.*

*5.) Then cometh he to a city of Samaria, which is called Sychar, near to the parcel of ground that Jacob gave to his son Joseph.*

*6.) Now Jacob's well was there. Jesus therefore, being wearied with his journey, sat thus on the well: and it was about the sixth hour.*

*7.) There cometh a woman of Samaria to draw water: Jesus saith unto her, Give me to drink.*

We have here the conversation between Jesus and this woman of Samaria who has come to the well. Although this situation starts at the well, Jesus ultimately wants to bring her into a place of true worship. The scriptures tell us in John 4:7 that this woman has come to draw water. Sometimes we are in situations that cause us to become dry. Sometimes we are in a dry place in our spiritual walk and we need to know how to draw from the well what we need to refresh our lives. When your water pot is empty and your bucket is dry, you need to know how come before the presence of the Lord to draw. The empty places in your soul, heart, life, and spirit can be filled. Therefore, Jesus waits for you at the well to fill your life again.

## "Give Me To Drink"

In John 4:7 the scripture says: ***"There cometh a woman of Samaria to draw water: Jesus saith unto her, give me to drink."*** When you are on your way from the well...to true worship, Jesus asks you to "give" him something. Many times, we come to church with the attitude of this woman at the well. We come to get something for ourselves. We come to Jesus for what we think we will receive from Him, but not always prepared to "give" Him something. Therefore, when Jesus asks something of us, we have a spiritual breakdown. Jesus has watched you put so much energy into satisfying yourselves that he wonders if you will make a sacrifice to satisfy Him. The church as a whole must get back to satisfying God. Think about it this way: in church, the preaching is to help us, the tithes and offerings we give are so we can be blessed, prayer time and alter calls are for us and our needs. Everything we do in church is for us, except "Praise and Worship." Praise and worship from our hearts is what we "give" to the Lord. We must get back to being pleasing to God. We must get back to being acceptable unto God. Instead of abusing the Lord's Name for a blessing; we must learn to bless His Name.

*John 4:9*

**9.) *Then saith the woman of Samaria unto him, How is it that thou, being a Jew, askest drink of me, which am a woman of Samaria? for the Jews have no dealings with the Samaritans.***

As this woman at the well talked with Jesus she begins to explain why she can't serve him. She explains that the Jews and the Samaritans don't deal with each other. And many times, we are the same way. We have our reasons as to why we cannot serve the Lord. Like this woman, we have our "excuses."

The woman goes on and on about Jesus not having his own water pot and trying to be greater that Jacob. Really, we are guilty of this too. We have all talked ourselves out of serving the Lord at some time. There is always a struggle between the flesh and the spirit, but we must be careful to yield the God's Spirit and His Word to overcome fleshly desires that come to steal that which is to be "given" to God: His praise and His worship.

Keep in mind that in this passage of scripture the Lord is taking us from the Well in verse 6; all the way to Worship in verse 24.

*John 4:10*

*10.) Jesus answered and said unto her, If thou knewest the gift of God, and who it is that saith to thee, Give me to drink; thou wouldest have asked of him, and he would have given thee living water.*

# "The Gift of God"

Another reason as to why many people don't pursue the Lord in passionate worship is because they don't know the gift of God. Just like this woman at the well, we can also have a subconscious resistance when it comes to engaging intimate encounters with the Lord. If we **"knew the gift of God"** and who He really is; it would prompt us to respond to Him in a more significant way.

We may know Bible stories; we may have memorized many Scriptures. We may know theological terms and Christian clichés. We may have great musicians, and superb stage presence. We can be intellectual, academic, and technical...**Yet, Still Not Know the Gift of God!**"

Think back on all the occasions that you have received gifts for. It could be anything from birthday presents to Christmas gifts. Even weddings, anniversaries, graduations are times when you most likely would have received a gift.

Depending on how long ago that was and how many times you were blessed, you don't really remember what all you received. You may even get a little confused as you try to remember which person gave you which gift. But what if someone give you a kidney, especially when your life depended on it? Let someone give you a gift that saves your life, and I guarantee that you will value the gift of life far above the money and material things. You would be far more thankful to the person whose gift saved your life, then a person who simply sent a "get well" card to you.

It's amazing that in our everyday life we can identify that which is the greater gift; and the same is true in worship. We must recognize Jesus as the gift of God. Jesus is the gift that God gave who saves and redeems our lives. When we really know the gift of God, we become inspired and motivated to love the one who first loved us. Therefore, our response to the gift is to love, serve, praise, and worship Him.

## "Are You Greater?"

*John 4:11-12*

*11.) The woman saith unto him, Sir, thou hast nothing to draw with, and the well is deep: from whence then hast thou that living water? 12.) Art thou greater than our father Jacob, which gave us the well, and drank thereof himself, and his children, and his cattle?*

This woman goes on and on about Jesus not having his own water pot, while questioning his significance in comparison to Jacob. Her first question is: "where do you plan on getting this water, seeing that you have no bucket to draw from the well?" Her follow-up question to that is: "are you greater than our ancestor Jacob who established this well?" She is basically asking Jesus "what makes you so great?"

This is an area we can be challenged in as well. We can become so busy, so common, and so consumed with our own lives to the point that we don't view God as being Great enough. Psalms 150 teaches us to praise him according to his "excellent greatness." Psalms 145:3 declares: "Great is the Lord, and greatly to be praised: and his greatness is unsearchable." **God is magnificent and there are no boundaries or limits to His Greatness**. True worshipers must have the ability to see God's greatness.

Jesus could have answered this one is questioned by saying: "yes, I am greater than your father Jacob." Jesus could have explained to her that He is in the direct lineage of Abraham Isaac and Jacob. Jesus could have addressed how He is the fulfillment of the prophecy that was spoken to Abraham by God. However, He chose to show compassion to give her more understanding.

*John 4:13-15*

*13.) Jesus answered and said unto her, Whosoever drinketh of this water shall thirst again: 14.) But whosoever drinketh of the water that I shall give him shall never thirst; but the water that I shall give him shall be in him a well of water springing up into everlasting life.*

***15.) The woman saith unto him, Sir, give me this water, that I thirst not, neither come hither to draw.***

Now, Jesus is explaining that it's not about the well of water in the ground; but it's a well of water that springs forth within us. Sometimes we are so empty in this life, that we search in natural, physical, and carnal "Wells" for solutions that are not there. We can be so empty in our souls, that we dig into earthly Wells, in the form of worldly pursuits, and fleshly desires. The tragedy is that all of those resources at some point dry up, and never bring the true fulfillment that they once promised. This is why we need the water that Jesus gives. The Water of his Spirit that satisfies us from within. We can receive the Water of His Spirit which is the well that never runs dry.

It is with this understanding that the woman at the well now responds to Jesus by saying, in verse 15: "Sir, give me this water, that I thirst no more, and neither come to this well to draw."

Seeing that her way of life has done nothing to fill the void or satisfy the emptiness of her soul; the woman at the well realizes that she needs the solution that Jesus brings. **It is in the place of emptiness that you have nothing to lose.** Even as believers there are times when we feel empty of God's presence, empty of purpose, empty of power, and empty of love. We could feel empty due to back-to-back struggles in life that drains us of our existence. True worship comes from a place of emptiness, because you really don't get all of Him - until you get rid of all of you.

Because in the place of emptiness you have nothing to give and nothing to prove. In this place of emptiness, we realize that enough is enough; and we come to understand that our lives are nothing as long as we are controlling it. It is in this place of emptiness that we say with all sincerity: "Lord, give me your water, that I thirst no more." It is in this place of emptiness that we make the commitment to no longer run to man-made sources in an attempt to fill a spiritual need.

Our thirst must shift from pleasing ourselves to pleasing the Lord. Our thirst and desire becomes expressed when we long to be filled with the Spirit of God, which is that Living Water. Just as it is quoted in the 23rd Psalm, we should desire our cups to run over as we are nourished and refreshed by the Lord.

## "Go, Call Your Husband"

*John 4:16-18*

*16.) Jesus saith unto her, Go, call thy husband, and come hither.*

*17.) The woman answered and said, I have no husband. Jesus said unto her, Thou hast well said, I have no husband:*

*18.) For thou hast had five husbands; and he whom thou now hast is not thy husband: in that saidst thou truly.*

After the woman asked Jesus for this Living Water, Jesus said, "Go call your husband." You need to understand that when you are on your way from the well to worship, Jesus will challenge you to "call your husband." When Jesus says, "Call your husband" he is really saying, "Show me who you are submitted and committed to." You cannot have true worship without submission. You cannot have true worship without a covering. True "covering" is what Adam and Eve the lost in the garden when they disobeyed the commandment of the Lord. They were covered in the light of God's glory; but that glory lifted from them when they were no longer submitted to the Will and the Word of God. Rebellion is an enemy to submission. That's why those who are living in rebellion to God cannot offer God true worship. Rebellion is as the sin of witchcraft... how can a witch worship God?

It is in the place of true worship that the light of God's glory is restored to our lives. When Jesus told the woman to call her husband, he was in fact calling her life into order. She then confessed to Jesus that she had no husband, and Jesus prophetically confirmed that she was true in her statement. Likewise, our lives will never come into true order until we are truthful concerning the condition of our lives. Jesus may be calling your attitude, motives, relationships, and lifestyle into order; will you respond in truth or will you lie to yourself?

The woman at the well indeed started this conversation in a more defensive posture, but is now very open and transparent with the Lord. **When Jesus asked the woman at the well to call her husband, he was really addressing her lifestyle of worship.** There is a deeper reason that I will explain as to why she had many husbands; and it has everything to do with her form of worship. This conversation was never about her personal life; but rather about her intimate encounter with Christ to usher her into the spirit of true worship.

## Intimate Encounters of Worship

*John 4:19-20*

*19.) The woman saith unto him, Sir, I perceive that thou art a prophet.*

*20.) Our fathers worshipped in this mountain; and ye say, that in Jerusalem is the place where men ought to worship.*

When Jesus confirmed this woman's truth concerning her husbands by mentioning details of her previous relationships (that He would not have known); she is now able to perceive that he is someone greater. She treated Jesus as a casual Jewish man at first. Now, that Living Water is starting to take effect and her perception of Jesus has changed. She now recognizes He is a Prophet. Once she is able to see Jesus on a higher level; the conversation also shifts to a higher level.

Many commentaries and theologians treat this part of the conversation as if the woman is trying to change subjects. Perhaps she is too embarrassed or convicted that Jesus has exposed her marital status. Many people view this Scripture as if she no longer wants to talk about husbands and boyfriends, and is trying to switch to something more spiritual because Jesus is a prophet. I submit to you however, the woman at the well is not changing subjects; but rather going deeper into the same subject. **Ever since Jesus asked for a drink of water, this conversation has been about worship...and not about her.** This woman is now able to connect all of the clues to see that the results of her natural life are parallel to the condition of her spiritual life. She has been living the wrong kind of life because she had the wrong understanding of worship. Her emptiness has now created a desire to know the truth. She is not challenging Jesus on the subject of worship; but rather seeking clarity as a result of receiving living water.

*John 4:21*

*21.) Jesus saith unto her, Woman, believe me, the hour cometh, when ye shall neither in this mountain, nor yet at Jerusalem, worship the Father.*

Jesus begins to explain that worship is no longer confined to a specific physical location. Worship is not based on customs and cultural expressions of past rituals. This is important because it is possible for people to hold the location so sacred that the purpose of worshiping God is overlooked. It is a false balance to have such a high commitment to the practice of

## "You Don't Know What You Worship"

*John 4:22*

> *22.) <u>Ye worship ye know not what</u>: we know what we worship: for salvation is of the Jews.*

In *verse 20*, the conversation at the well begins to shift more toward the object of worship. Worship had been a controversial subject between Jews and Samaritans. The woman understood that her forefathers worshipped in "this mountain" and yet the Jews said that Jerusalem was the place where worship was to take place. Even to this day there are those who still debate about worship, where to worship, methods of worship, styles of music, the use musical instruments, and on and on. Yet, in the middle of Jesus correcting her lack of understanding, He went so far as to tell her that she didn't even know what she worshipped. Let me ask you a question and give you the answer.

**The question is**: "Why did Jesus tell the woman she did not know what she worshiped?"

**The answer is**: "<u>Because she was a Samaritan</u>."

Think about it for a moment, none of the Samaritans "know" what they worship, because they worship so many things. The act of worship in Samaria was no longer pure due to a strong presence of idolatry and compromise.

To understand this, you must have some knowledge of Israel's history. There was a time when the nation (the 12 tribes) was divided. There were 10 tribes that formed the Northern Kingdom. The two remaining tribes, Judah and Benjamin, formed the Southern Kingdom. The Northern Kingdom was referred to as "Israel," while the Southern Kingdom was referred to as "Judah." For hundreds of years these two kingdoms would have war and conflict.

Samaria was the capital of the Northern Kingdom of Israel. This location was situated in a well-nourished Valley.

*1 Kings 16:21-24*

*21.) <u>Then were the people of Israel divided into two parts</u>: half of the people followed Tibni the son of Ginath, to make him king; and half followed Omri.*

*22.) But the people that followed Omri prevailed against the people that followed Tibni the son of Ginath: so Tibni died, and Omri reigned.*

*23.) In the thirty and first year of Asa king of Judah began Omri to reign over Israel, twelve years: six years reigned he in Tirzah.*

*24.) <u>And he bought the hill Samaria of Shemer for two talents of silver, and built on the hill, and called the name of the city which he built, after the name of Shemer, owner of the hill, Samaria</u>.*

Here we see Omri, the seventh king of Israel come into power. It is King Omri that purchased the land that he would establish as Samaria. Samaria was not only a city, but also the name of the region that surrounded that area. The problem, however, is the fact that Omri was a wicked king that did evil in the eyes of God; and caused Israel to follow in his evil ways.

*1 Kings 16:25-26*

*25.) But Omri wrought evil in the eyes of the LORD, <u>and did worse than all that were before him</u>.*
*26.) For he walked in all the way of Jeroboam the son of Nebat, and <u>in his sin wherewith he made Israel to sin</u>, to provoke the LORD God of Israel to anger with their vanities.*

Omri died after he had reigned as king for twelve years, which allowed his son Ahab to take the throne. As King, Ahab also continued to do evil and live wickedly, even more so than his father Omri. In addition to that, he married Jezebel and embraced the worship of Baal.

*1 Kings 16:30-32*

*30.) And Ahab the son of Omri did evil in the sight of the LORD above all that were before him.*

*31.) And it came to pass, as if it had been a light thing for him to walk in the sins of Jeroboam the son of Nebat, that he took to wife Jezebel the daughter of Ethbaal king of the Zidonians, and went and served Baal, and worshipped him.*

*32.) <u>And he reared up an altar for Baal in the house of Baal, which he had built in Samaria</u>.*

When King Omri built Samaria, it became a place of great wickedness. Under the rulership of King Ahab, Samaria now becomes a place dedicated to the worship of Baal. But even in all of that, it's only the beginning.

## Intimate Encounters of Worship

*2 Kings 17:24-33*

*24.) And the king of Assyria brought men from Babylon, and from Cuthah, and from Ava, and from Hamath, and from Sepharvaim, and placed them in the cities of Samaria instead of the children of Israel: and they possessed Samaria, and dwelt in the cities thereof.*

*25.) And so it was at the beginning of their dwelling there, that they feared not the LORD: therefore the LORD sent lions among them, which slew some of them.*

*26.) Wherefore they spake to the king of Assyria, saying, The nations which thou hast removed, and placed in the cities of Samaria, know not the manner of the God of the land: therefore he hath sent lions among them, and, behold, they slay them, because they know not the manner of the God of the land.*

*27.) <u>Then the king of Assyria commanded, saying, carry thither one of the priests whom ye brought from thence; and let them go and dwell there, and let him teach them the manner of the God of the land</u>.*

*28.) Then one of the priests whom they had carried away from Samaria came and dwelt in Bethel, and taught them how they should fear the LORD.*

*29.) <u>Howbeit every nation made gods of their own</u>, and put them in the houses of the high places which the Samaritans had made, every nation in their cities wherein they dwelt.*

*30.) And the men of Babylon made Succothbenoth, and the men of Cuth made Nergal, and the men of Hamath made Ashima,*

*31.) And the Avites made Nibhaz and Tartak, and the Sepharvites burnt their children in fire to Adrammelech and Anammelech, the gods of Sepharvaim.*
*32.) So they feared the LORD, and made unto themselves of the lowest of them priests of the high places, which sacrificed for them in the houses of the high places.*

*33.) <u>They feared the LORD, and served their own gods</u>, after the manner of the nations whom they carried away from thence.*

These Scriptures record how the King of Assyria had invaded and took possession of the land of Samaria. The Assyrians then brought in people from

Babylon and other surrounding regions to inhabit the land of Samaria. But keep in mind, that these foreigners also brought with them their foreign gods, which only adds more wickedness to the idolatry that's already present in the land of Samaria.

There was a point when the king of Assyria realized that the Israelites no longer knew their own God (verse 27); and actually, sent a priest to teach them the ways of the Lord. However, in the process of this time, the people of Israel who continued to inhabit Samaria became mingled with the foreigners in marriage and in worship. As they were being taught the ways of the Lord, the children of Israel then began to mix the laws of the Torah with the practice of idolatry.

The idolatry practiced in Samaria would also include the killing children as human sacrifices. Another practice of idolatry in Samaria would consist of groups gathering for the purpose of being sexually promiscuous among themselves. This perversion was a part of their idol worship. That's the deeper reason as to why the Woman at the Well had many husbands in her life. But, it's not just this woman's way of life. This is common among all the inhabitants of Samaria.

Samaria had come to the place of no longer being pure in race, neither pure in religion. Samaria is a place where the people worship anything and everything. The Scriptures even talk about how people began to make their own gods. Can you imagine that? A place where people serve the Lord while serving other gods. That's Samaria!

Jesus told the woman at the well (a woman of Samaria), that she did not know what she worshiped. Now, that you understand some biblical history of Samaria, you can see why she would have been misguided in her practices and in her understanding of worship.

When Jesus spoke to the woman at the well concerning her five husbands by asking her to call for her husband; he was bringing to her awareness the fact that she had no one to call on. Jesus was not singling her out to expose her personal business. This woman's lifestyle was common among all the men and women of Samaria. Even if Jesus had spoken to a "man at the well," that man would have had the same struggle if Jesus challenged him to go call his wife.

What about us? Are we Samaritans? As people who claim to have the Lord, what have we mixed and mingled into our lifestyles that are not pleasing to

God? What idolatry, wickedness, or false practice have we mixed into our faith and worship?

What traditions do we practice? What superstitions do we believe? What other pledges and oaths are we bound by, while claiming to be in covenant with the true living God?

## "In spirt and in truth"

*John 4:23-24*

*23.) But the hour cometh, and now is, when the true worshippers shall worship the Father in spirit and in truth: for the Father seeketh such to worship him.*

*24.) God is a Spirit: and they that worship him must worship him in spirit and in truth.*

The woman at the well showed great passion for worship. Jesus only needed to correct her understanding. Think about this. This woman's worship was rooted in performing from the flesh, based on false beliefs. She was performing works of the flesh because she was dedicated to a false religion. Jesus had to call her away from what was of the **"flesh"** and away from a belief that was **"false."**

The opposite of "flesh and false" is **"spirit and truth."** Those who worship the Father, must worship Him in spirit and in truth; not in flesh rooted in something false. Before entering into true worship, the Lord has to correct any distorted view you may have of what worship is.

Sometimes we look at how people conduct their church services and say, "That's how they worship." Sometimes we here different types of music and say, "That's how they worship." The only problem is that Jesus said, "True worshippers shall worship the Father in **spirit and in truth**." Did you realize in this passage of scripture, the subject of worship is not associated with "music?"

Praise is a word in scripture that is very often associated with Music, Singing, Dancing, and Rejoicing. Worship, isn't! We know the Bible teaches us to "Sing Praises" to the Lord but how do you "Sing Worship?" Psalms 150 instructs us to "Praise" him with musical instruments and in the dance not "Worship" him with instruments and the dance." Why do we think that worship means to sing slow songs? Why do we put such a musical emphasis on worship when the scriptures do not?

## Intimate Encounters of Worship

Of course, that doesn't mean that we cannot worship Him while being musical. Neither am I suggesting that music can't be used to express worship. The point is simply to get into a place in our walk with God where He corrects our view of what we think worship is. You cannot give God "true worship" if you don't even know what it is! You cannot please Him if you don't know what He likes! Worship is not just for Sunday morning service, it's for life! Worship is anytime, every time, and all the time.

Before you experience true worship, Jesus will meet you at **"Your Well."** The well is where the Lord confronts you. It is the place where you become exposed to yourself. It is the place where you are called back to God's order and purpose. The well is where God prepares you for true worship. You will not reach true worship if you have not first been by the well. God gets the sin out of your life at the well. God crucifies your flesh at the well. You must be washed at the well before you can worship in His presence, and then you will have something to offer when the Lord says, "Give me to drink."

* Worship does not come from the flesh.

* Worship does not come from fashion and formalities.

\* Worship does not come from performance and activity.

\* Worship does not come from programs.

\* Worship does not come from religious rituals.

\* Worship is not come from man-made traditions.

Worship comes from your **spirit** when you are able to embrace the **truth** of who God is.

*...God is a Spirit: and they that worship him must worship him in spirit and in truth.*

# Chapter 3:

## "Lifestyle of Radical Worship"

In this chapter I want to share with you some principles of scripture that can help us understand what God expects of His worshippers. We must know the standard God has set for the lifestyle of the worshipper. Even though we have freedom and liberty in Christ Jesus, we are not at liberty to go against God's Holy Standard. Let's read these two passages of scripture as we explore the subject of worship.

### Worship Principle # 1: "Avoid the Error of Flesh in Worship"

*II Samuel 6:1-7*

1.) *Again, David gathered together all the chosen men of Israel, thirty thousand.*

2.) *And David arose, and went with all the people that were with him from Baale of Judah, to bring up from thence the ark of God, whose name is called by the name of the Lord of hosts that dwelleth between the cherubims.*

*3.) New cart, and brought it out of the house of Abinadab that was in Gibeah: and Uzzah and Ahio, the sons of Abinadab, drave the new cart.*

*4.) And they brought it out of the house of Abinadab which was at Gibeah, accompanying the ark of God: and Ahio went before the ark.*

*5.) And David and all the house of Israel played before the LORD on all manner of instruments made of fir wood, even on harps, and on psalteries, and on timbrels, and on cornets, and on cymbals.*

*6.) And when they came to Nachon's threshing floor, <u>Uzzah put forth his hand to the ark of God</u>, and took hold of it; for the oxen shook it.*

*7.) And the anger of the LORD was kindled against Uzzah; and <u>God smote him there for his error;</u> and there he died by the ark of God.*

We see here as 2 Samuel begins, the recovering of the Ark of God (His Presence). The Ark was placed on a new cart pulled by oxen. While the Ark was being transported the oxen stumbles, which causes the cart and the ark to shift so greatly that it appears as if it will fall. Uzzah, in an attempt to keep the Ark from falling, puts his hands on the Ark to secure it. In doing so, the wrath of God killed Uzzah right on the spot. The interesting thing is that verse 7 says that God killed Uzzah for his "**error**" and he died by the Ark.

So, there's a clue here for us to be careful that we do not handle God's presence in error.

What was the error? Well, for one, the Ark was to be carried by the priests not pulled by animals. Secondly, the Ark was not to be physically touched in that manner; but rather, carried by the staves that were to be placed within the rings of the Ark.

But, let me offer another perspective on what the error was. The Ark was representative of the "Presence" of God. The word "presence" in the Hebrew language means "Face" or "Face to Face." Uzzah put his hands on the Ark; meaning he put his "Hand" in God's "Face." How disrespected do you feel when someone puts his/her hand in your face?

Also notice this, Uzzah used human flesh to help God's Presence; but God declared that no flesh will "glory" in His presence. The Presence of God and the flesh of man do not mix. Uzzah teaches us how important it is for us to crucify our flesh and deny ourselves. Uzzah teaches us that "Carnal" or "Fleshy" people are not welcome in the presence of God. He teaches us to respect God and not to put our hands (flesh) in his face.

This means that it is time to purify and cleanse whatever you may have in your life that is not like a God.

You will not be able to stand, stay, or dwell in the presence of God; living by the flesh and carnality. Worship is not done by the flesh but it is done in spirit and in truth.

Uzzah teaches us that God deals seriously with those who mishandle His Glory, His Presence, and His Authority!

...And many churches (figuratively) have "Dead Uzzahs" in the congregation:

- -Dead to the shifting of the atmosphere.
- -Dead to the anointing.
- -Dead with no spiritual awareness.
- -Dead to a new move of God.
- -Dead with no liveliness in praise.

## **Worship Principle # 2: "Be Afraid"**

*2 Samuel 6:8-9*

> 8.) *And David was displeased, because the LORD had made a breach upon Uzzah: and he called the name of the place Perezuzzah to this day.*
>
> 9.) <u>*And David was afraid of the LORD that day*</u>, *and said, How shall the ark of the LORD come to me?*

Maintaining respect for God's power is the beginning of wisdom and the process of perfecting holiness in the fear of God. 2 Samuel 6:9 talks about how David was afraid of the Lord that day, and asked: **"How shall the ark of the Lord come unto me?"** David was afraid because he did not expect God to kill someone for doing a "good thing." There was music, dancing and rejoicing for the recovery of the Ark. Everything seemed to be in order, but the death of Uzzah confused David. Sometimes we may be doing things that seem to be okay in worship, yet God disapproves. It is dangerous to believe that God's power and presence meets us on our terms. David then asked the question that we must also ask: "How shall the Ark of the Lord come to me? In essence; how do I carry myself, to be able to carry God's Glory and Presence?"

Seeing the death of Uzzah was the wakeup call that let David know they were doing something wrong! We should be able to look and see when there is a dead Uzzah (or too much Flesh) within the ministry. Even the church praise & worship Ministry can become a "Dead Uzzah." The live band and the voices of the choir can become a Dead Uzzah.

That's because the even though we are active in our expressions, it's not based on human effort. We must be able to carry the responsibility of what means to be worshippers. Real worship is not limited by a person's skill level or talent in the field of music. Just because you can carry a tune, doesn't mean that you can carry the Ark or carry the Weight of His Glory! Just because you can hold a note, doesn't mean that you can uphold the Anointing and responsibility of the Priesthood! Examine your heart posture towards God. That's where true worship comes from.

Are we too confident in our own ways? Or are we afraid enough to enquire as David did: how we should **Carry His Glory?**

* How we should handle this Ministry?

* How we should treat the Anointing?

\* How am I to Handle my **role as a Royal Priesthood**?

Sometimes we are challenged to overcome the culture, traditions, habits, methods and ways that keep us from truly abiding in the presence of the Lord. And though these things may carry a personal significance, they are not a necessity for worship. Therefore, we must follow the example of King David, and be willing to unlearn the ways we have assumed to be acceptable. **We must return to the heart of worship; which is intimacy and communion with the Lord.**

## <u>Worship Principle #3</u> "Prepare to Move"

*2 Samuel 6:10-12*

> 10.) *So David would not remove the ark of the LORD unto him into the city of David: but David carried it aside into the house of Obededom the Gittite.*
>
> 11.) *And the ark of the LORD continued in the house of Obededom the Gittite <u>three months</u>: and the LORD blessed Obededom, and all his household.*

12.) *And it was told king David, saying, The LORD hath blessed the house of Obededom, and all that pertaineth unto him, because of the ark of God. So David went and brought up the ark of God from the house of Obededom into the city of David with gladness.*

As a result of Uzzah's death and the revelation of the fact that they were mishandling the Ark of God; verses 10 & 11 says that: "David would not remove the Ark for 3 Months."

Sometimes it's good for a Leader to do like David, and shut down that area of Ministry to allow time for people to get things right (not just winging it). It is better for a position to remain vacant, than to have to replace an Uzzah who has embarrassed the whole ministry!

Take a real good Look at Uzzah in this chapter, and you'll see that his actions:

*1. Brought an end to the celebration,*

*2. Wasted the efforts of everyone who had taken the time to prepare for that day,*

*3. Caused a time delay of 3 months,*

*4. Kindled the anger of the Lord.*

*5. Had everybody sad at what was supposed to be a joyous occasion,*

*6. And had King David questioning the Lord.*

David took the time to get new people, get a new strategy and move in a new direction. During the three months while the Ark as in the home of Obed Edom, David restructured everything. He appointed the priests who would carry the ark. David along with other leaders of the tribes appointed singers, musicians, ministers, and porters. They even changed their wardrobe. This was something that was far grander than the days when Moses did it; and it was all for the Glory of the Lord.

## **Worship Principle # 4: "Sacrifice"**

*2 Samuel 6:13*

> *13.) And it was so, that when they that bare the ark of the LORD had gone six paces, <u>he sacrificed oxen</u> and fatlings.*

Also, in 2 Samuel 6:17, the Ark is brought to the "Tabernacle of David," where sacrifices were made. It is ironic that oxen were used to pull the Ark, when perhaps they would have been better served as the sacrifices before the Ark. The point to be made here is: Don't try to pull on God's presence with things that should be sacrificed.

When developing a lifestyle of radical worship, one must understand the meaning of the word "Worship." The Hebrew meaning of "Worship" is to "Kiss" or to "Kiss Toward." It is the mark of close friendship. To kiss someone is nothing like a hand shake, for we shake the hands of strangers. To kiss someone is nothing like hugging, yet we hug those we are more familiar with. The kiss, however, is for someone you are "very close" to or very intimate with. The kiss is for someone with whom there is a strong relationship. So, is it possible to live so close to God that we can kiss his face in worship? How do we develop this intimacy and closeness with the Lord?

In General, it has been said that our relationship with God has been more for seeking His "Hand" rather than seeking His "Face." In essence we care more about what He has for us than who He is to us. In our reading, we see recorded in 1 Chronicles 16:11; the fact that we should "seek his face continually." In the life of the radical worshipper, it's all about who God is, and not necessarily what God does. Yet we learn more about who He is through His mighty acts and deeds.

## Worship Principle # 5: "Radical Worship can be Despised"

*2 Samuel 6:14-23*

*14.) And David danced before the LORD with <u>all his might</u>; and David was girded with a linen ephod.*

*15.) So David and all the house of Israel brought up the ark of the LORD with shouting, and with the sound of the trumpet.*

*16.) And as the ark of the LORD came into the city of David, Michal Saul's daughter looked through a window, and saw king David leaping and dancing before the LORD; and she despised him in her heart.*

*17.) And they brought in the ark of the LORD, and set it in his place, in the midst of the tabernacle that David had pitched for it: and David offered burnt offerings and peace offerings before the LORD.*

*18.) And as soon as David had made an end of offering burnt offerings and peace offerings, he blessed the people in the name of the LORD of hosts.*

19.) *And he dealt among all the people, even among the whole multitude of Israel, as well to the women as men, to every one a cake of bread, and a good piece of flesh, and a flagon of wine. So all the people departed every one to his house.*

20.) *Then David returned to bless his household. And Michal the daughter of Saul came out to meet David, and said, How glorious was the king of Israel to day, who uncovered himself to day in the eyes of the handmaids of his servants, as one of the vain fellows shamelessly uncovereth himself!*

21.) *And David said unto Michal, It was before the LORD, which chose me before thy father, and before all his house, to appoint me ruler over the people of the LORD, over Israel: therefore will I play before the LORD.*

22.) *And I will yet be more vile than thus, and will be base in mine own sight: and of the maidservants which thou hast spoken of, of them shall I be had in honour.*

23.) <u>*Therefore Michal the daughter of Saul had no child unto the day of her death*</u>*.*

In *verse 16*, David's wife despised him in her heart. It's amazing how you can have all that celebration, praise and worship going on, and still have people who won't enter in or participate. They sit there and watch what's going on as if "**all this is really not necessary.**"

There are people who will sit right in church, and despise you the whole time you're ministering. They might say: "God bless you" to your face; but in their heart they despise you. The truth is, people who fall into this category are not rejecting you; but rejecting the presence of the Lord.

In *verse 22:* Davis says, if you think I look foolish praising God now, you better not blink; because you haven't seen nothing yet. I am going to irritate you even more because I'm going to pursue God in ways more "Radical" than this.

David teaches us, not to allow our praise to be governed or hindered by people who choose not to enter in. It is also interesting to note in verse 23: that Michal (*David's wife*), as a result of her attitude and her actions against David's worship; became barren.

Which teaches us another powerful principle: **"Those who Don't Praise Don't Produce!"**

If your lifestyle is not a life of praise that actively peruses the presence of God; it will not produce.

-You won't produce an Intimate Encounter!

-You won't produce His Glory!

-You won't produce His Anointing.

-You won't produce His Power!

-You won't produce any Change in the Atmosphere!

### **Worship Principle # 6:** "Seek His Face"

*I Chronicles 16:1-11*

*1.) So they brought the ark of God, and set it in the midst of the tent that David had pitched for it: and they offered burnt sacrifices and peace offerings before God.*

*2.) And when David had made an end of offering the burnt offerings and the peace offerings, he blessed the people in the name of the LORD.*

*3.) And he dealt to every one of Israel, both man and woman, to every one a loaf of bread, and a good piece of flesh, and a flagon of wine.*

*4.) And he appointed certain of the Levites to minister before the ark of the LORD, and to record, and to thank and praise the LORD God of Israel:*

*5.) Asaph the chief, and next to him Zechariah, Jeiel, and Shemiramoth, and Jehiel, and Mattithiah, and Eliab, and Benaiah, and Obededom: and Jeiel with psalteries and with harps; but Asaph made a sound with cymbals;*

*6.) Benaiah also and Jahaziel the priests with trumpets continually before the ark of the covenant of God.*

*7.) Then on that day David delivered first this psalm to thank the LORD into the hand of Asaph and his brethren.*

*8.) Give thanks unto the LORD, call upon his name, make known his deeds among the people.*

*9.) Sing unto him, sing psalms unto him, talk ye of all his wondrous works.*

*10 .) Glory ye in his holy name: let the heart of them rejoice that seek the LORD.*

***11.) Seek the LORD and his strength, seek his face continually.***

We must focus on seeking the Face of the Lord continually. Matthew 6:33 says: "But **seek** ye first the kingdom of God, and His righteousness; and all these things shall be added unto you." The word "seek" means in the Greek ***to inquire of, and to desire.*** Think about how that definition enlarges our understanding of "Seeking" first the Kingdom. In other words, my **first desire** is to be for God, His rulership, and His righteous ways. Have you gotten to the place where your first desire is for God? How strong is your desire for His righteousness? How strong is your desire for His presence?

David makes a powerful statement in Psalms 27:4 which reads: "One thing have **I desired** of the Lord, and that will **I seek** after; that I may dwell in the house of the Lord all the days of my life, **to behold the beauty** of the Lord, and **to inquire** in his temple." David discovers one thing worth desiring, one thing worth seeking after, and that is the beauty of the Lord (His Presence). The Lord doesn't hesitate to give you the desire of you heart when He is the desire of your heart. **As you seek the Lord in worship, the Lord is seeking you as a worshipper.**

Do you realize that Satan is fighting against God because of "Worship?" Lucifer, the one-time anointed Cherub was cast out of Heaven over his issues with God concerning who should be worshipped. Look at Lucifer's actions as recorded in the book of Isaiah.

*Isaiah 14:12-15*

*12.) <u>How art thou fallen from heaven, O Lucifer</u>, son of the morning! How art thou cut down to the ground, which didst weaken the nations!*

*13.) For thou hast said in thine heart, I will ascend into heaven, I will exalt my throne above the stars of God: I will sit also upon the mount of the congregation, in the sides of the north:*

*14.) I will ascend above the heights of the clouds; I will be like the most High.*

*15.) Yet thou shalt be brought down to hell, to the sides of the pit.*

Ever since Lucifer's failed attempt to be the one to receive more worship than the Most-High God, his mission has been to simply to turn man's worship to anything but God. He does this through distractions, oppression, false religion, false doctrine, temptations, deception, and feeding man's fleshly desires. Satan tempted Adam and Eve to eat of the forbidden fruit to interrupt their lifestyle of worship. In the Garden of Eden, Adam and Eve were in the presence of the Lord "continually" and since Satan has been cast out of the presence of God; it is obvious that he doesn't want anyone else dwelling in the presence of God.

### <u>Worship Principle #7</u>: "Don't Worship for Things"

*Matthew 4:8-11*

*8.) Again, the devil taketh him up into an exceeding high mountain, and sheweth him all the kingdoms of the world, and the glory of them;*

*9.) And saith unto him, All these things will I give thee, if thou wilt fall down and worship me.*

*10.) Then saith Jesus unto him, Get thee hence, Satan: for it is written, Thou shalt worship the Lord thy God, and him only shalt thou serve.*

*11.) Then the devil leaveth him, and, behold, angels came and ministered unto him.*

Take note of the fact that the devil said to Jesus: "...***<u>All these things will I give thee</u>***, *if thou wilt fall down and worship me."*

If you recall in *Matthew 6:33*, Jesus taught that as you seek first the Kingdom of God and his righteousness... then "***All these things***" shall be added unto you. This shows us that even the devil is aware of God's desire to bless those who worship Him. One of the devil's tactics is to give people good gifts, or good opportunities, yet his purpose is to distract your worship away from God.

Jesus demonstrated to us that he was able to resist the devil's offer they responded by saying:

*"...Thou shalt worship the Lord thy God, and him only shalt thou serve."*

It was at this point that the devil realized he had no influence over the worship of Christ. it is extremely frustrating to the devil when we are not deterred and remain undistracted in our lifestyle of radical worship. As a result of Jesus not giving in to Satan's temptations, *verse 11* says that the devil left him. The same is true for us. A lifestyle of radical worship is a torment to the devil. This is how we are able to show the devil that he has no place in our lives. God's provisions are always greater than Satan's temptations.

# Chapter 4:

## "The King of Glory Shall Come In"

*Psalm 24:1-2*

*1.) The earth is the LORD'S, and the fulness thereof; the world, and they that dwell therein.*

*2.) For he hath founded it upon the seas, and established it upon the floods.*

Ok, I want you to stop and think about how awesome that Is. First of all, we live on the Earth. We view the earth as something solid, (which it is). The Earth is solid in the fact that it is not a liquid or a gas. The Earth, however, is miraculously founded upon the seas and established on the floods.

You know, when we build a structure, we are careful to build on solid ground. Jesus even said that a wiseman would build his house on a rock; meaning a firm foundation. In building and construction, if a foundation is not firm or solid; it can compromise the entire structure that is built upon it. That is not the case, however, when it comes to God. He used the **"waters of the sea" as a foundation for the Earth.**

*Genesis 1:1-2, 6-10*

*1.) In the beginning God created the heaven and the <u>earth</u>.*

*2.) And the earth was without form, and void; and darkness was upon the face of the deep. And the Spirit of God <u>moved upon the face of the waters</u>.*

*6.) And God said, <u>Let there be a firmament in the midst of the waters</u>, and let it divide the <u>waters from the waters</u>.*

*7.) And God made the firmament, and <u>divided the waters which were under the firmament from the waters which were above the firmament</u>: and it was so.*

*8.) And God called the firmament Heaven. And the evening and the morning were the second day.*

*9.) And God said, <u>Let the waters</u> under the heaven be gathered together unto one place, <u>and let the dry land appear</u>: and it was so.*

*10.) And God called the dry land <u>Earth</u>; and the gathering together of the waters <u>called he Seas</u>: and God saw that it was good.*

The waters which at first covered the Earth, and rendered it unfit to be a habitation for Man; were ordered under it. This was done that the dry land might appear. Thus, the waters became a foundation.

The Earth is the Lord's. The Lord made it and formed it. He founded it, and He fitted it for the use of man. The matter is His, though it was made out of nothing. The Form is His, completely made according to the eternal counsels of His own mind. He is the only, complete, and the absolute owner. The Lord founded the Earth upon the seas and upon the floods.

One would probably view the waters of the sea as a weak and unstable foundation to build the Earth on. But the Lord, Almighty, shall bear the weight of this Earth by His own Word.

Hebrews Chapter 1 tells us that He upholds all things by the Power of His Word. Even for the believers; the Word of the Lord is our foundation. Yet the Word of God is also water. This we know because as the Bride of Christ, we are washed in the "Water of His Word."

**The Earth is the LORD'S, and he hath founded it upon the seas, and established it upon the floods.**

---

*Psalms 24:3*

*3.) Who shall ascend into the hill of the LORD? Or who shall stand in His holy place?*

Do you have the ability to ascend into the hill of the Lord? As the presence of the Lord is rising, true worshippers can rise with Him. As the King of Glory draws near, Kingdom People will have already prepared the Way.

Consider that Jerusalem geographically sits on a hill about 2,300 feet above sea level. Therefore, when going to Jerusalem, you must go "up" (or in essence, you must ascend into the Hill of the Lord). The same is true in the life of the believer. As we embrace the King of Glory, we must be prepared to ascend. We must be prepared to rise!

...Arise and shine for the Light is come; and the glory of the Lord is risen upon you. Yes, He is the King of Glory, but the glory of the Lord is also upon you. Keep in mind King David had to reset the order as to who should handle the Ark of God. The Levites were appointed to bear the Ark.

## Exodus 32:26

*26.) Then Moses stood in the gate of the camp, and said, Who is on the LORD'S side? let him come unto me. <u>And all the sons of Levi gathered</u> themselves together unto him.*

## Deuteronomy 10:8

*8.) At that time the LORD separated the tribe of Levi, to bear the ark of the covenant of the LORD, to stand before the LORD to minister unto him, and to bless in his name, unto this day.*

The Levites were the ones originally assigned to handle The Ark of God and to minister in the Holy Place. The Levites were the ones originally assigned to serve as the Priesthood. In 1 Chronicles 15, David reestablishes the Priests as the ones to bear the Ark. Even David himself was dressed like a priest when they proceeded in recovering the Ark of God. Likewise, look what Christ has done to position us as believers:

## 1 Peter 2:5

*5.) Ye also, as lively stones, are built up a spiritual house, an holy priesthood, to offer up spiritual sacrifices, acceptable to God by Jesus Christ.*

## 1 Peter 2:9

*9.) But ye are a chosen generation, a royal priesthood, an holy nation, a peculiar people; that ye should shew forth the praises of him who hath called you out of darkness into his marvellous light:*

Through Christ, we become a Holy and Royal Priesthood. Therefore, we gain access to ascend into His presence and stand as ministers in His Holy Place. We offer up spiritual sacrifices and show forth His praises!

*Who shall ascend into the hill of the LORD? Or who shall stand in His holy place?*

The answer to that question is found in the following verse.

*Psalm 24:4-5*

*4.) He that hath <u>clean hands</u>, and a <u>pure heart</u>; who hath not <u>lifted up his soul</u> unto vanity, nor <u>sworn deceitfully</u>.*

*5.) He shall receive the blessing from the LORD, and righteousness from the God of his salvation.*

Don't forget what David said in *I Chronicles 15:12*: *"...sanctify yourselves, both ye and your brethren, that ye may bring up the ark of the LORD God of Israel unto the place that I have prepared for it."*

The Lord requires "purity" from those who ascend into His Holy presence. When the scripture says: **"He that has clean hands"**, it is speaking of an outward, practical holiness. This person keeps their hands from doing that which is evil. A person with "clean hands" will study the Word of God diligently to know what God requires; and then refuse to participate in that which is contrary to the Word of God. The aim is to live in a way as to keep clean hands.

Think about when Jesus was on trial. Pilate knew that the Lord was innocent and yet he gave in to the overwhelming cry to crucify Him. Pilate also knew his deed would dirty his hands. Therefore, he tried to wash his hands in water to maintain his integrity and innocence.

According to Psalms 24, standing in the Lord's presence is not only about maintaining clean hands but also having a "Pure Heart." Not only must your hands be pure; but more importantly, your hearts must be pure.

**"...Blessed are the pure in heart: for they shall see God."** (Matthew 5:8)

## Intimate Encounters of Worship

It is possible for a person to be outwardly righteous, (having clean hands), but not inwardly righteous, (having clean hearts). In Matthew 23:27, Jesus call these types of people: "hypocrites." Jesus said they were like "whited sepulchers" which indeed appear beautiful outwardly; but are inwardly full of dead men's bones, and of full of all uncleanness.

While man looks on the outside God looks at the heart. A hypocrite is, in some ways, worse than one who has unclean hands; because hypocrites disguise their motives.

One who ascends unto the hill of the LORD must keep his heart pure, cultivate sincerity, and give priority to what God sees - rather than what man sees.

In moving beyond the clean hands, and the pure heart, there is also the responsibility of having a lifestyle of proper worship. One who desires to ascend unto the hill of the LORD does not lift up their soul unto vanity. That is, he or she doesn't place any trust and affections in idols and false worship. Idols are lifeless and powerless; therefore, it is vain to seek after or trust in idols. Anyone therefore, who pursues after idols, demonstrates disdain for God by foolishly worshipping something of man's own imagination.

The root word of imagination is "image." It is the fallen nature of mankind that always creates a false image. God alone is our Creator. He alone is the Living and True God and deserves our affections.

Those who ascend into the presence of the Lord; are people who have properly placed their worship on the Lord. They deal honestly both with God and man. In their covenant with God and their agreements with men; they have not sworn deceitfully, nor broken their promises.

They have not violated their engagements, nor taken any false oaths. Without regard to the obligations of truth or the honor of God's nature, we are unfit for a place in God's Holy hill. Uzzah did not have "clean hands," But Obededom did.

*Psalm 24:6-7*

*6.) This is the generation of them that seek him, that seek thy face, O Jacob. Selah.*

*7.) Lift up your heads, O ye gates; and be ye lift up, ye everlasting doors; and the King of glory shall come in.*

After the category 5 Hurricane Michael ripped through my city with massive destruction; the President of the United States came to the city.

But before the President arrived, the Secret Service was already here. They always travel ahead of the President to ensure the safety and the security of the path that the President is to take. Therefore, some of the hurricane clean-up that took place; did not happen for us as the residents...it was actually for the arrival of the President. **Because, his presence demands that the pathway be cleared.**

This same principle is true for our Lord, but in a far greater measure! His presence demands that the pathway be cleared for His arrival.

...And when that path is open, The King of Glory Shall Come In.

King Jesus is our King of Glory. We should continually maintain a clear path for the presence of the King in our Lives. **It is possible, that you are not experiencing the true power and presence of the King; because you have not completely cleared the pathway.**

You are the dwelling place where the King desires to abide. You are the temple, but the key to experiencing a greater manifestation of God's glory in your life depends on your ability to **prepare the way of the Lord.**

> **"Lift up your heads, O ye gates; and be ye lift up, ye everlasting doors; and the King of glory shall come in."**

The reality is that every gate must be opened and every door must be lifted up!

### This meaning has many layers:

**1.** Those who were assigned to the gates of the city were **to lift their heads and be alert** as the Ark of God enters the city.

**2.** Seeing that the Lord desires to dwell/abide within us; we allow our gates to **lift our heads to the Lord.**

And these gates determine what we discern and perceive. They determine what we since around us.

**\* We have an Eye Gate.**

In the natural, when something catches our eye, we most often will lift up our heads.

**\* We have an Ear Gate.**

In the natural, when sound catches our ear, we will lift up our heads.

**\* We have a Nose Gate.**

In the natural, if we smell something, we will lift up our heads.

\* **We have a Mouth Gate.**

In the natural, when we attempt to speak loudly or proclaim something, we will naturally lift our heads.

We pretty much understand this idea of the gates; but it's the door that is often left unclear. We don't always connect the "Lifting Up" of doors to anything practical as it relates to our relationship to the Lord. For the most part; doors don't lift up. Doors usually open in and out. Doors easily open side to side. I mean, yes there's a garage door that can be lifted up. Yes, there's a fancy car door that can be lifted up. These, however, still don't do it justice; until we remember:

*1 Chronicles 15:1.*

*1.) And David made him houses in the city of David, and prepared a place for the ark of God, and <u>pitched for it a tent</u>.*

It is an act of worship to "prepare a place for the Ark." Let every heart – prepare Him room. As believers with a heart of worship, it is our sincere desire to be the "living temple" and dwelling place of God. Have you pitched your life as a tent? Have you purposed to live your life as a prepared place for the Lord?

Also take notice that this scripture informs us that David set up a tent for the Ark of the Lord. Can you visualize in your mind that The Ark was about to arrive to a large **tent**? The King of Glory was approaching a **tent**. In the Bible days, if you want to keep the doors of a tent open; they must be **"lifted up."**

\* According to **1 Chronicles 15:18;** Obededom was appointed to be a "porter" for the Ark of God!

\* According to *1 Chronicles 15:24;* Obededom was appointed to be a **"Door Keeper"** for the Ark of God!

The Porters (in scripture) were the one that were **called upon to "open the doors."** Likewise, we have to lift "our doors" to receive the King of Glory.

I want to challenge you today to lift up your door, as a dwelling place for the Spirit of God. However, this is not a revolving door, an automatic door, nor a screen door. **This is an "Everlasting Door."** In other words, once you open your door for the King of Glory; that door is to remain lifted and open forever!

They are called everlasting doors for a reason. That's how you transition from a tent to a temple. As tents that have housed the Glory of God for a season, God is calling us to shift from the state of being temporary - to becoming a permanent dwelling place.

If you will commit to being lifting up as an everlasting door; the King of Glory shall come in.

* The King of Glory comes in with <u>Power</u>!

* The King of Glory comes in with <u>Strength & Might</u>!

* The King of Glory comes in with <u>Victory</u>!

* The King of Glory comes in <u>Defeating Every Enemy</u>!

The government shall be upon His shoulders, and of His Kingdom shall be no end. His thrown is forever. He is the King Eternal.

Now, do you remember that David inquired of the Lord as to how he should recover the ark? Do you remember David leaving the Ark at Obededom's house for three months?

Here in the 1 Chronicles 15; we have another account of the same event. But this chapter gives us a behind-the-scenes look at what David was doing during those three months and while preparing for the recovery the ark.

### I Chronicles 15:12-14

*12.) And said unto them, Ye are the chief of the fathers of the Levites: <u>sanctify yourselves</u>, both ye and your brethren, that ye may bring up the ark of the LORD God of Israel unto the place that I have prepared for it.*

*13.) For because <u>ye did it not at the first</u>, the LORD our God made a breach upon us, for that we sought him <u>not</u> after the due order.*

*14.) So the <u>priests and the Levites sanctified themselves</u> to bring up the ark of the LORD God of Israel.*

"Sanctify yourselves" so that you will be able to usher in the presence of the Glory! Sanctification is a vital key for your spiritual walk as you prepare for the King of Glory!

That verse 3 reference stating: "Because ye did it not at the first" is reflecting on the events of Uzzah (who had touched the Ark of God). David reminds the people that they had messed it up the first time.

Sanctify means to be "set apart" or "separated" for a specific purpose." You can't usher in the King of Glory without being sanctified. Sanctifying yourself is a lifestyle change, and it is necessary to fulfill the assignment. A Lifestyle change that includes getting rid of distractions. A Lifestyle change that includes getting rid of worldliness.

A Lifestyle change that includes getting rid of sin and the weight that besets us. Preparing for the King of Glory means that we commit to staying pure for the Lord's purpose by living a sanctified life!

*Psalm 24:7-10*

*7.) Lift up your heads, O ye gates; and be ye lift up, ye everlasting doors; and the King of glory shall come in.*

*8.) Who is this King of glory? The LORD strong and mighty, the LORD mighty in battle.*

*9.) Lift up your heads, O ye gates; even lift them up, ye everlasting doors; and the King of glory shall come in.*

*10.) Who is this King of glory? The LORD of hosts, he is the King of glory.*

There are three levels of God's manifestation in the Earth:

Level 1 = is The Kingdom

Level 2 = is The Power

Level 3 = is The Glory

This is a journey that leads to an intimate encounter with the King of Glory that compels us to be everlasting doors. **Our lives are to be a never-ending invitation** for the presence of the Lord dwelling in our hearts. We often pray it when we quote **Matthew 6:13:**

*13.) ...For thine is the Kingdom, and the Power, and the Glory, forever. Amen.*

# Chapter 5:

## "Worship the King"

<u>Matthew 2:1-11</u>

*1.) Now when Jesus was born in Bethlehem of Judaea in the days of Herod the king, behold, there came wise men from the east to Jerusalem,*

*2.) Saying, <u>Where is he that is born King of the Jews</u>? for we have seen His star in the east, <u>and are come to worship him</u>.*

*3.) When Herod the king had heard these things, he was troubled, and all Jerusalem with him.*

*4.) And when he had gathered all the chief priests and scribes of the people together, he demanded of them where Christ should be born.*

*5.) And they said unto him, In Bethlehem of Judaea: for thus it is written by the prophet,*

*6.) And thou Bethlehem, in the land of Juda, art not the least among the princes of Juda: for out of thee shall come a Governor, that shall rule my people Israel.*

*7.) Then Herod, when he had privily called the wise men, enquired of them diligently what time the star appeared.*

*8.) And he sent them to Bethlehem, and said, Go and search diligently for the young child; and when ye have found him, bring me word again, that I may come and worship him also.*

*9.) When they had heard the king, they departed; and, lo, the star, which they saw in the east, went before them, till it came and stood over where the young child was.*

*10.) When they saw the star, they rejoiced with exceeding great joy.*

*11.) And when they were come into the house, they saw the young child with Mary his mother, <u>and fell down, and worshipped him</u>: and <u>when they had opened their treasures</u>, <u>they presented unto him gifts</u>; gold, and frankincense, and myrrh.*

<u>Matthew 2:2</u>

*2.) Saying, Where is he that is born King of the Jews? for we have seen His star in the east, and are come to worship him.*

### Intimate Encounters of Worship

This is your invitation to come and worship the King! We should worship Him because God created us to have fellowship with Him. This book has expressed that one of the most powerful ways to commune with the Almighty God; is through the art and the act of worship.

Worship is not necessarily a time when you are asking God for something; but is it time with Him...simply because He is God. Praising God is done because of "what He does for you." Worshipping God is done because of "who He is to you." Worship, when it is done in spirit and in truth; is something God can't ignore!

Worship in "spirit" signifies that your flesh must die. The flesh of man's carnal nature is not something acceptable in the sight of God as true worship. Start with the truth of who God is! If we have the wrong understanding, wrong concept/Idea, or the wrong motives; our worship will not be True Worship!

For the believer, worship should be easy and natural because we were created to worship.

Worship is a place where we acknowledge Christ as the center of our lives. When the wise men came into the house, Jesus was immediately the "Center" of their attention and the center of their worship. Be

Christ centered, not self-centered! You have to acknowledge Jesus at the center of it all!

When you worship Him with all of your heart just because you love Him; He fills the room with His presence, His love, His strength, and His power. That's how you are changed, from glory to glory.

Worship is a time for you to express to the Lord the true sentiments of your heart: how you trust Him, how you need Him, and how much you love Him.

The only thing in worship that matters, is that God is pleased. God is pleased when you have laid everything at His feet; and have offered your worship is a sweet fragrance to His nostrils.

———

*Matthew 2:11*

> *11.) And when they were come into the house, they saw the young child with Mary his mother, and <u>fell down, and worshipped him</u>: and when they had opened their treasures, they presented unto him gifts; gold, and frankincense, and myrrh.*

When people approached Kings in biblical times; they would kneel and bow. This posture represents being humble before the Lord.

If the people did not come to the king with this kind of humility, most likely; they would be killed. People would come to see the King for various reasons:

...Some, hoping for a favor to be extended to them, especially if they have wronged the king. An earthly king had the option of putting them to death, putting them in prison, or banishing them from the Kingdom. On the other hand, the king could grant them a pardon, or in some way honor the request.

So, if an earthly king has the ability to do something favorable for man; how much more does the King of Glory have the ability to bless us, if we humble ourselves in His presence?

### *Psalms 95:6 Reads:*

*6.) O come, let us worship and bow down: let us kneel before the LORD our maker.*

The latter part of Matthew 2:11 says:

*"...and when they <u>had opened their treasures</u>, they presented unto him gifts; gold, and frankincense, and myrrh."*

Worship is the place where you open your treasures. It is the place where you present your gifts. So, present and give yourself as "Gold" as you are purified and refined in the fire of God.

Give yourself as "Frankincense" which is the sweet fragrance created by your lifestyle of worship. Present and give yourself as "Myrrh" being dead to the world and the flesh, by being made alive again in Christ!

## Chapter 6:

### "The Conclusion"

The Lifestyle of being a true worshipper is the key to being an everlasting door. It is that attitude of extreme reverence for the Lord that persuades us to live as sinless as humanly possible. Yet, in the event that we do sin, we are quick and sincere in our repentance.

David teaches us a powerful truth about worship that we sometimes don't give enough attention to. In the scriptures, we first learn of the Ark of God when Moses was given the pattern and instructions for the Tabernacle from the Lord. In that Tabernacle there were three main sections. The first is the "Outer Court." The second is the "Inner Court". The third is the "Holy of Holies." In the days of the Tabernacle of Moses, only the High Priest was permitted to enter beyond the veil into the Holy of Holies where the Ark of God was housed. Only the High Priest could minister before the Lord in presence of the Ark of God.

Anyone not properly ordained of the Lord to enter that place would die for their error.

So, the question is this. If King David was not a High Priest, how did he get the Glory and Presence of God to manifest on the Ark? How was King David able to enter the Lord's presence without consequences? The answer is "WORSHIP." King David found another way into the presence of God by which we had not been introduced sense the days of Moses. David teaches us this principle that praise and worship produces a pathway into God's presence.

*Psalm 100:2*

*2.) Serve the LORD with gladness: come before his presence with singing.*

You can sing your way into the presence of God. The Heavenly Father seeks worshippers and there is no more veil of separation between God and Mankind. Once we are committed to the Lord Jesus Christ, expressing praise and worship becomes a way of life.

Even in those private moments in the tent that was pitched for the Ark, King David experienced the manifestation of the Lord's presence upon the Ark of God. As the Light of God's Glory appeared upon the Ark, a shadow was cast from the Cherubim that were on the Mercy Seat. David being in a posture of kneeling and bowing beneath the Ark gives us insight as to how he was able to "abide under the shadow" of the Almighty.

*Psalm 91:1*

*1.) He that dwelleth in the secret place of the most High shall abide under the shadow of the Almighty.*

We become the everlasting open door. Our praise produces the pathway for His presence. Our worship creates an atmosphere that serves as a secret place, and in the presence of the Lord – is the fulness of joy. This is what an Intimate Encounter of Worship produces in the lives of worshipping believers. Now, imagine how much greater it will be when the Lord returns and we see Him as He is…Face to Face, In All His Glory!

*Jude 1:24-25*

*24.) Now unto him that is able to keep you from falling, and to present you faultless before the presence of his glory with exceeding joy,*

*25.) To the only wise God our Saviour, be glory and majesty, dominion and power, both now and ever. Amen.*

www.ingramcontent.com/pod-product-compliance
Lightning Source LLC
LaVergne TN
LVHW040157080526
838202LV00042B/3198